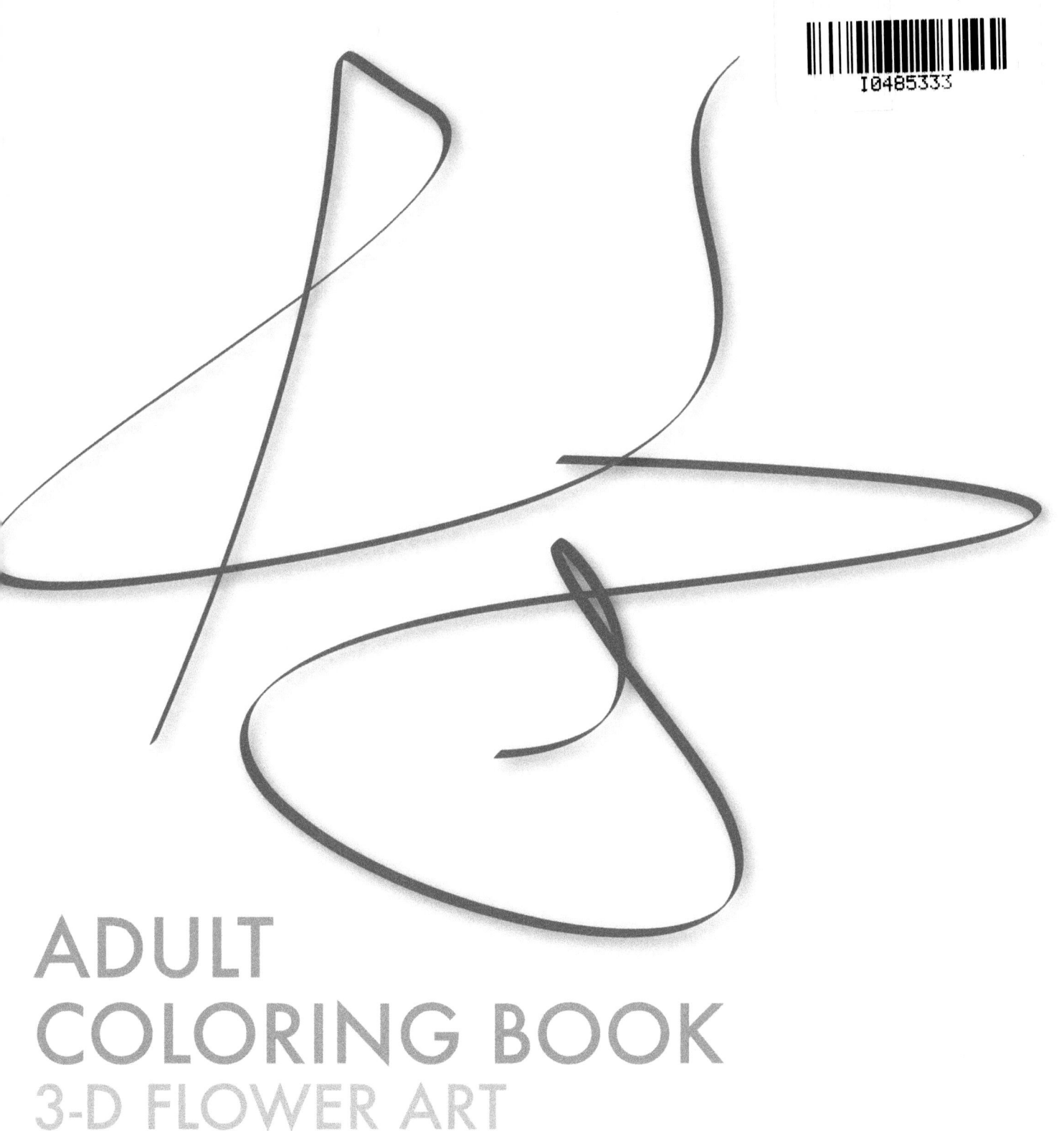

# ADULT
# COLORING BOOK
## 3-D FLOWER ART

BY DARRELL MITCHELL II

# COPYRIGHT

# DEDICATION

*I Dedicate this book to my kids, Macayla, Siara,*

*Mavi'e, & Maceo.*

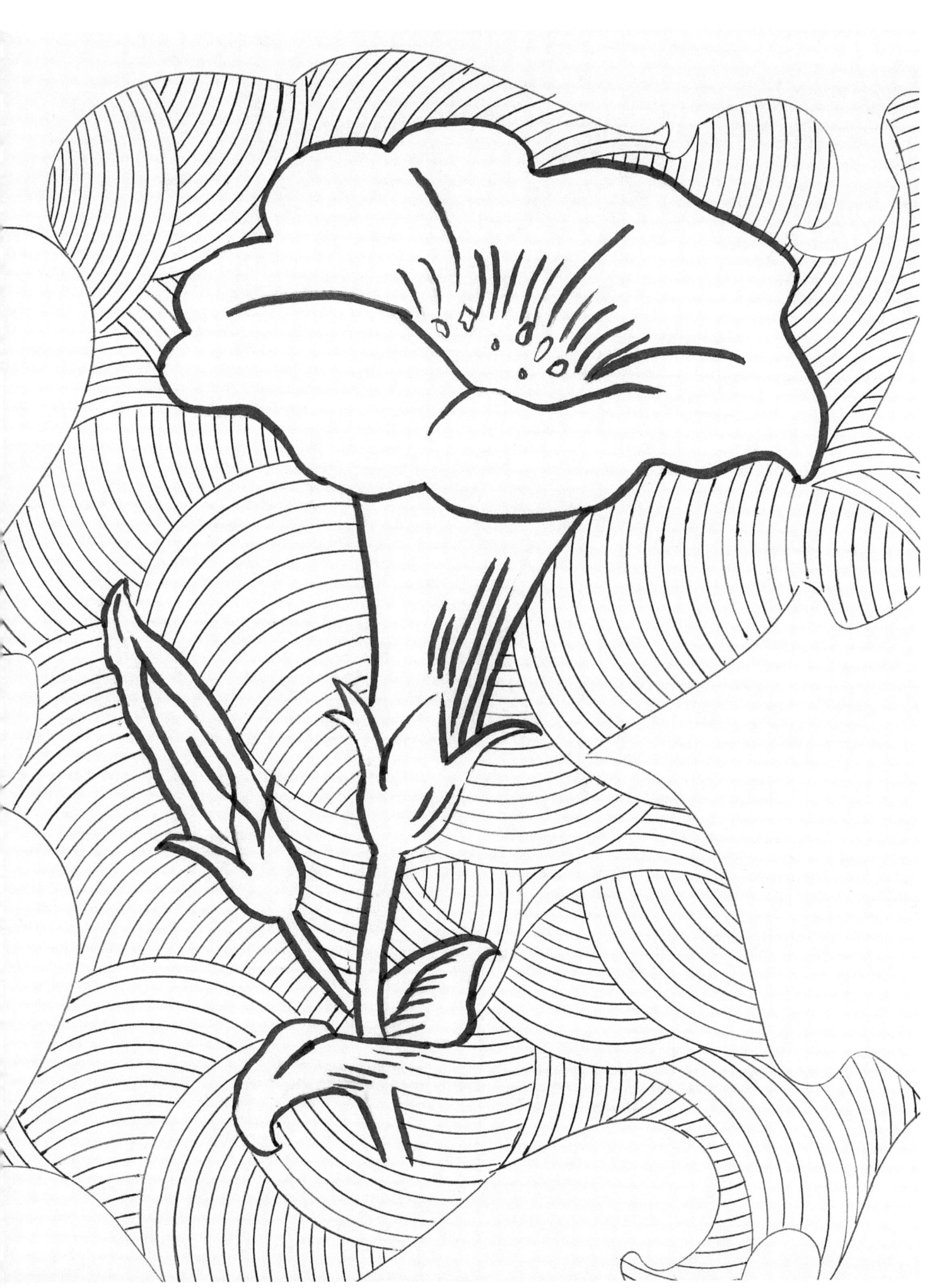

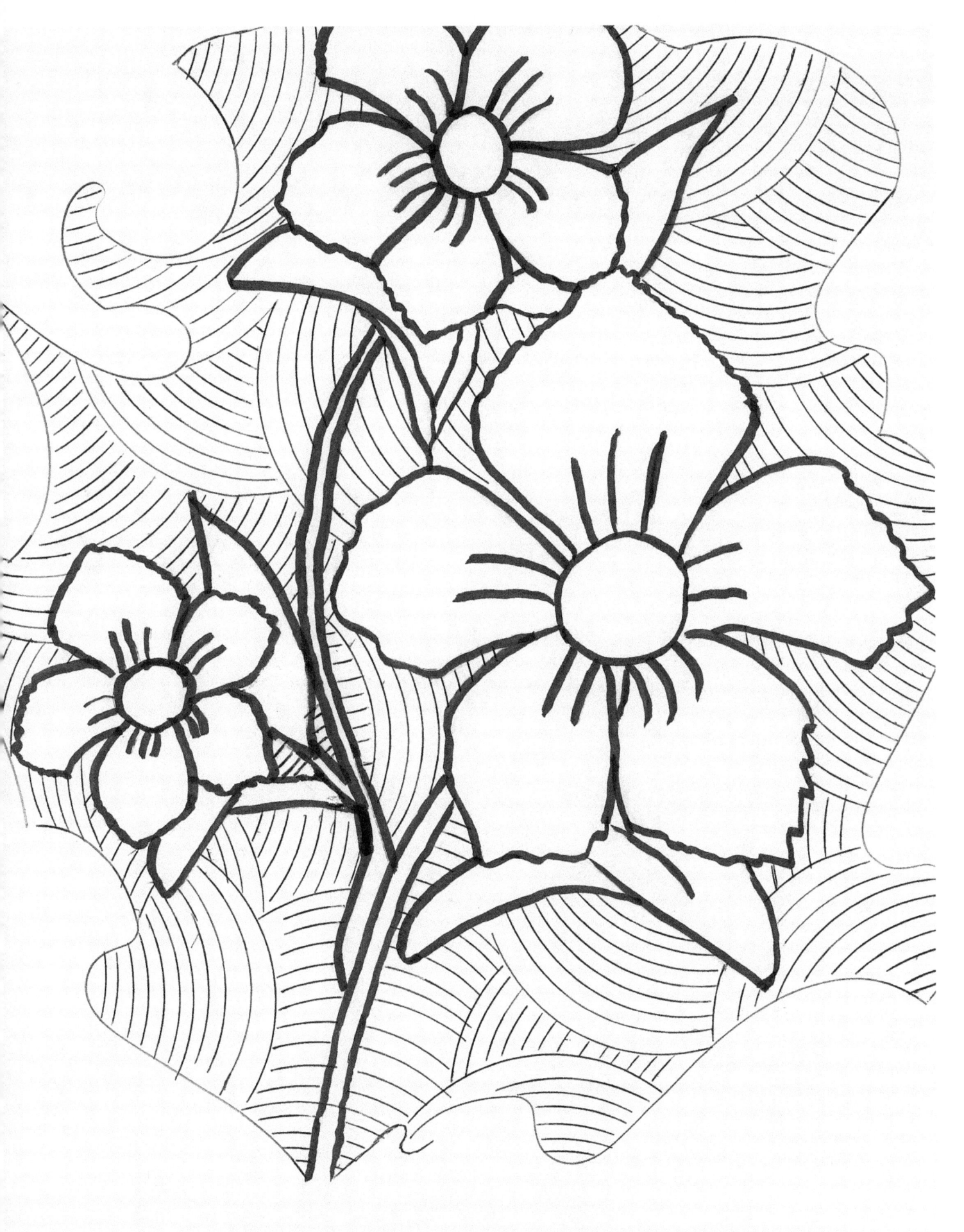

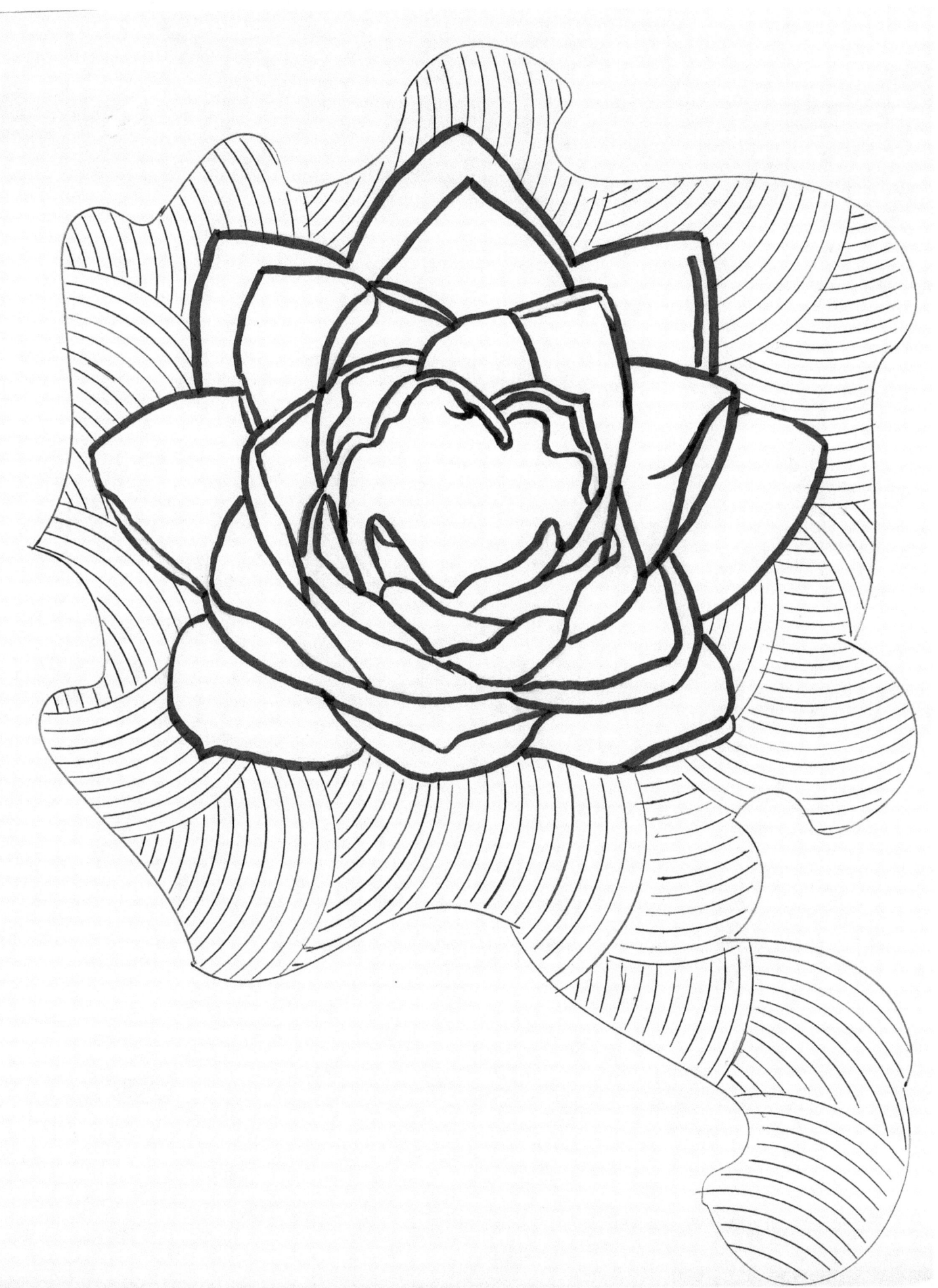

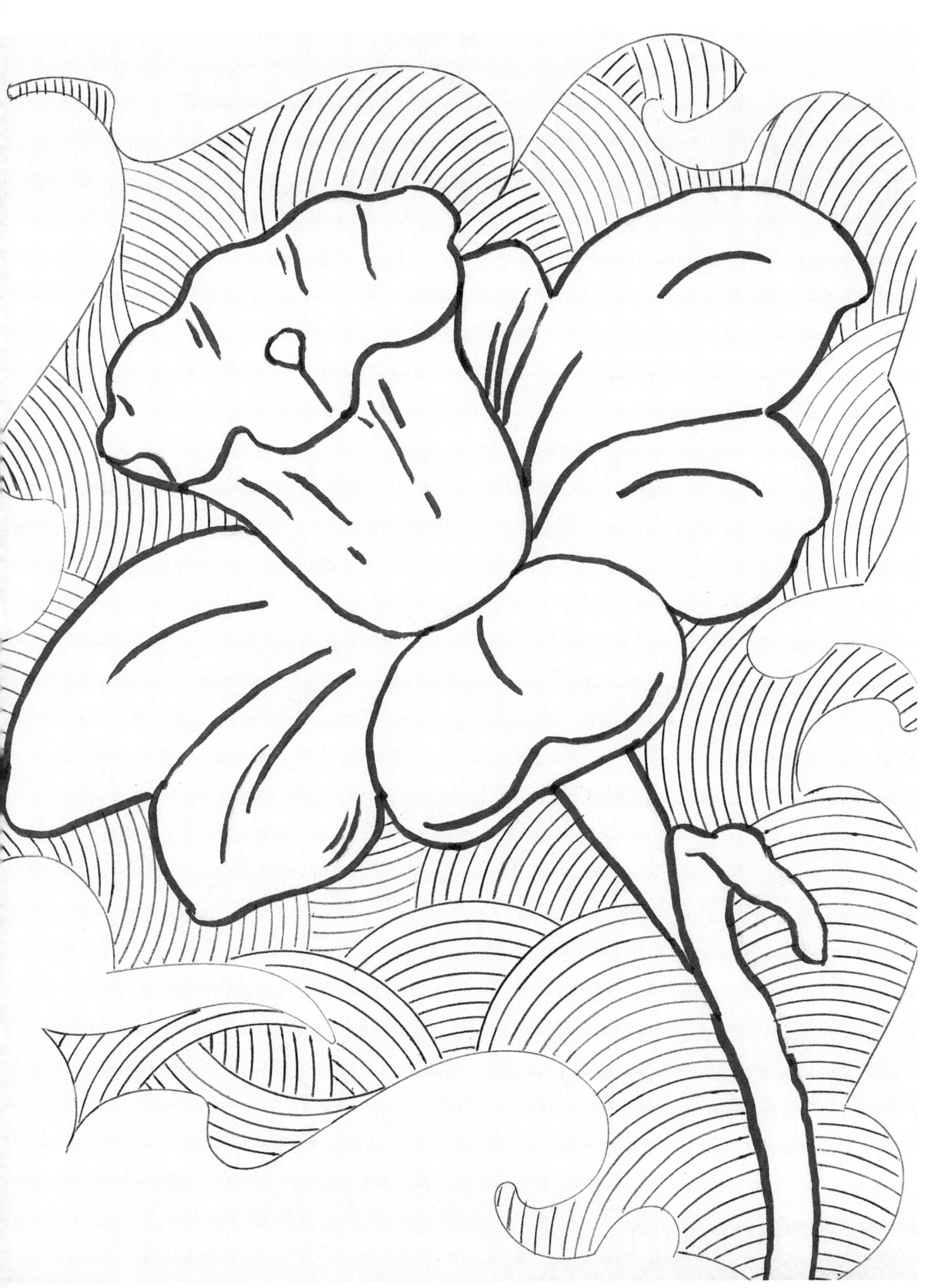

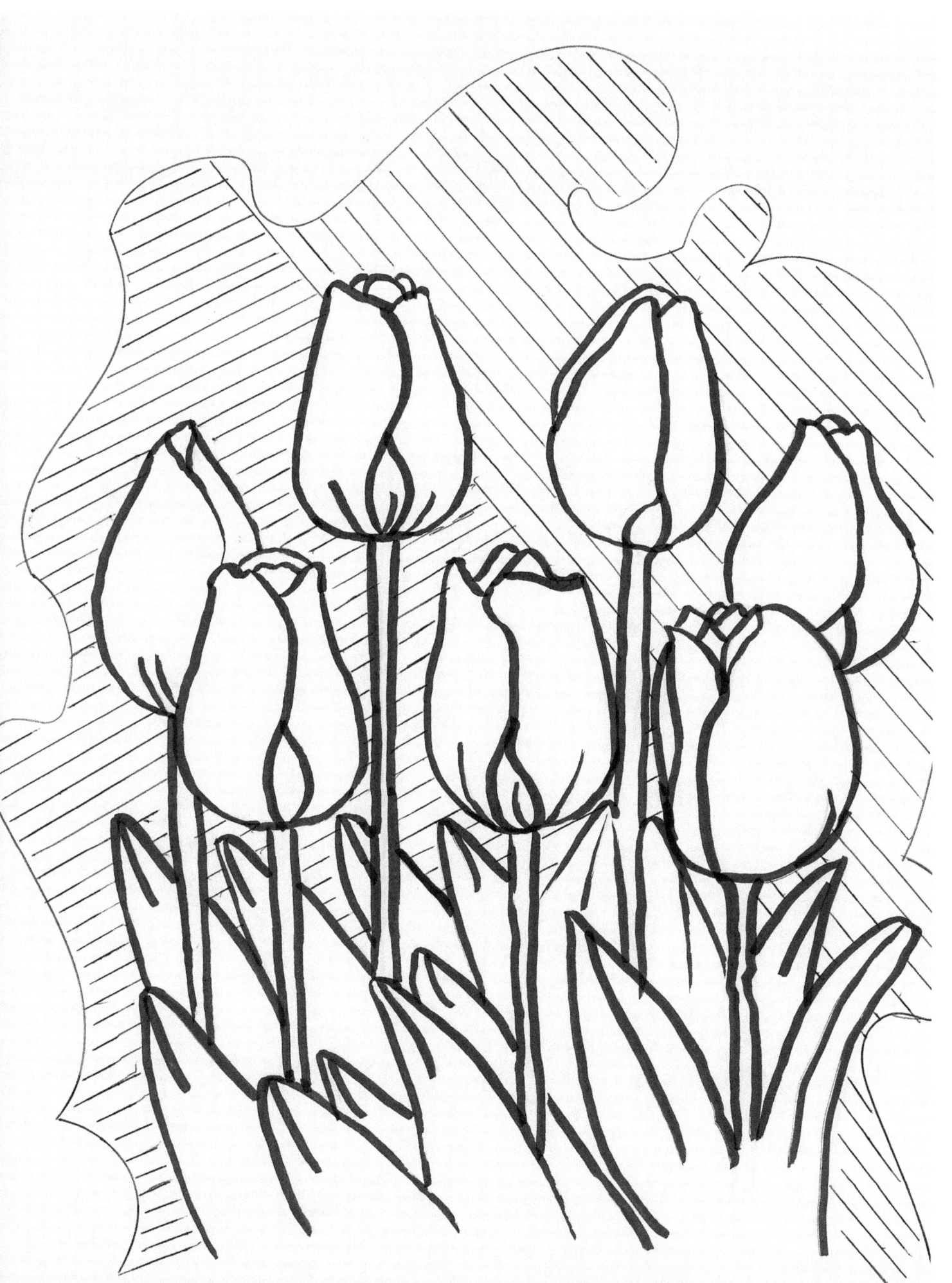

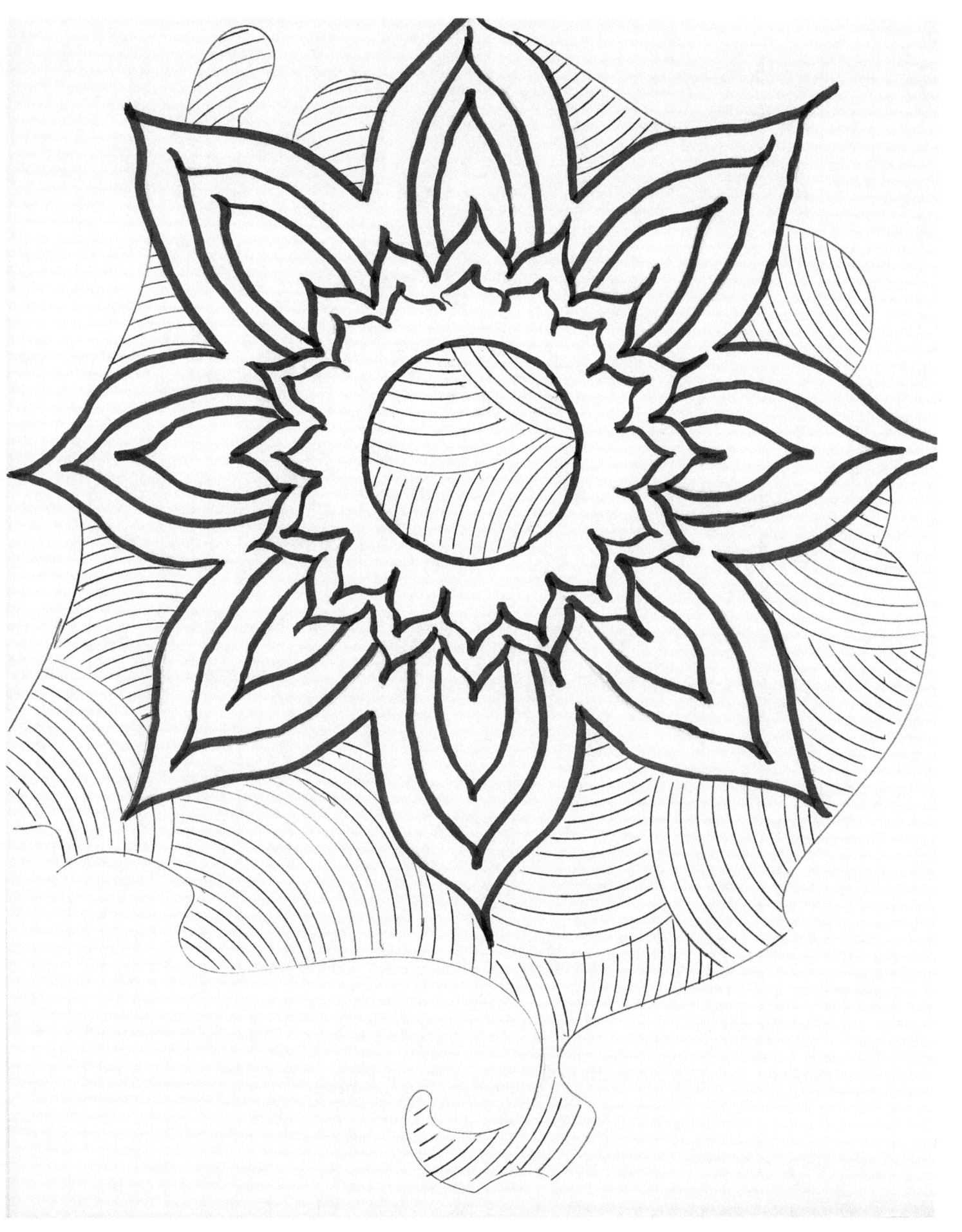

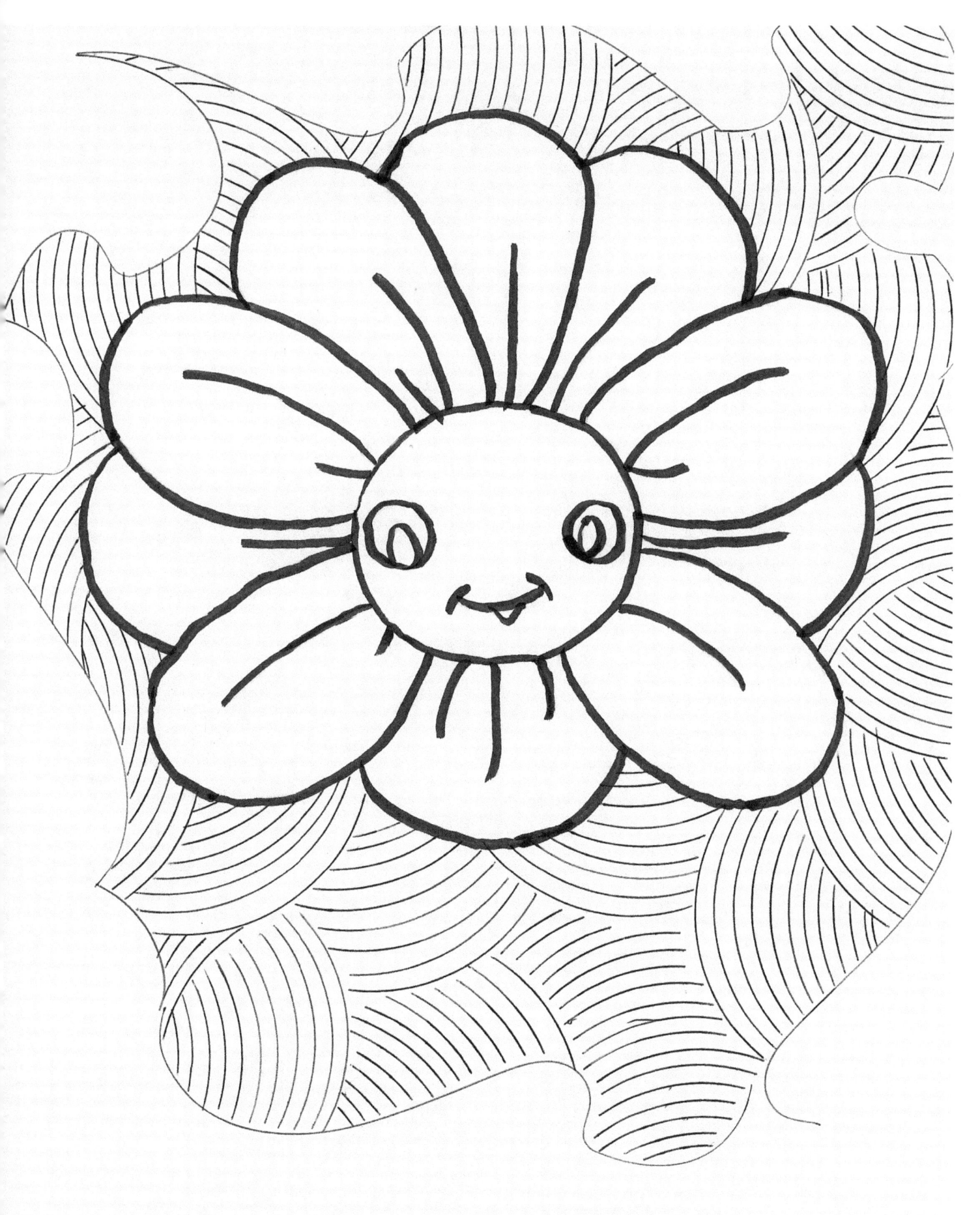

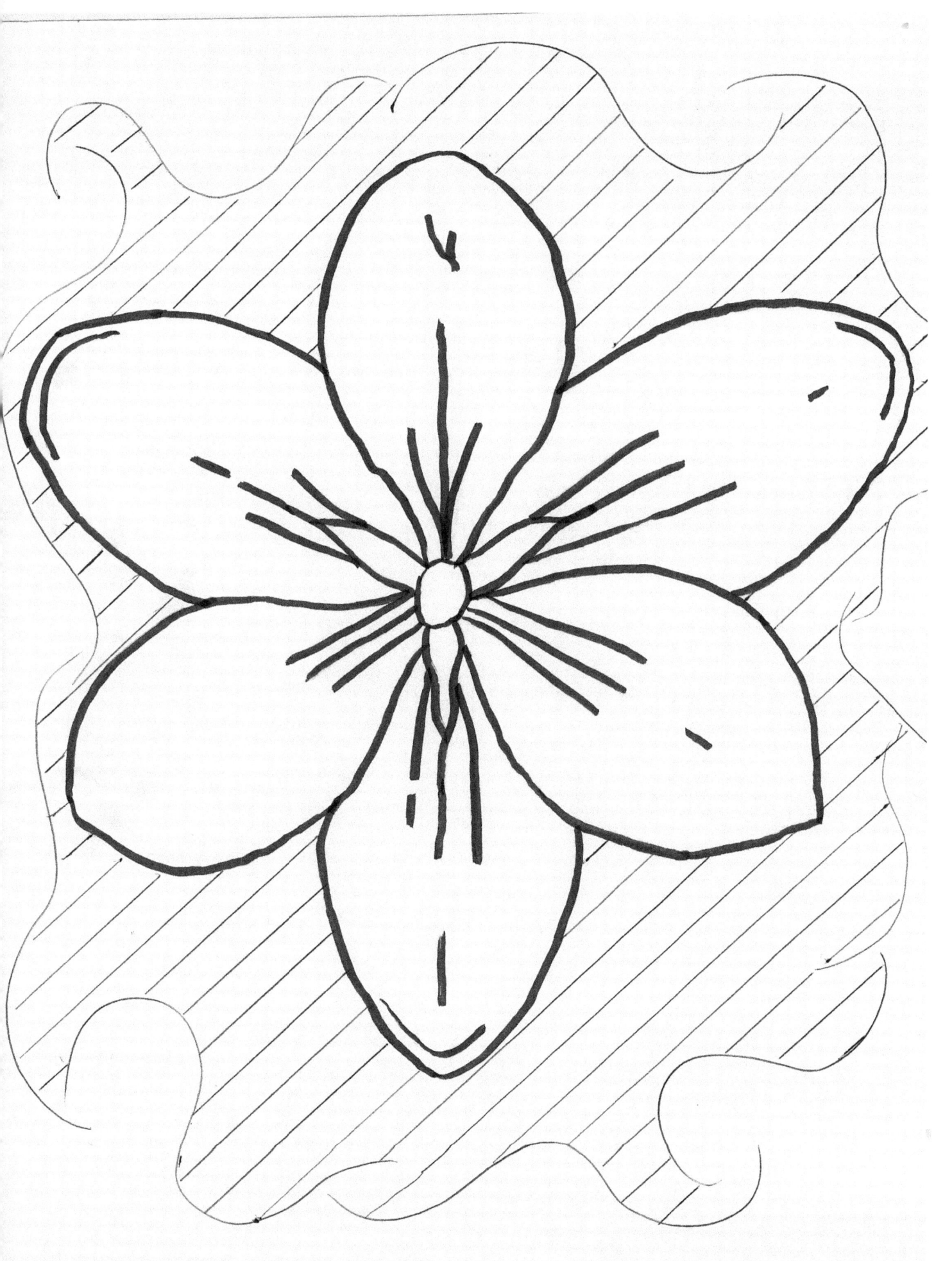

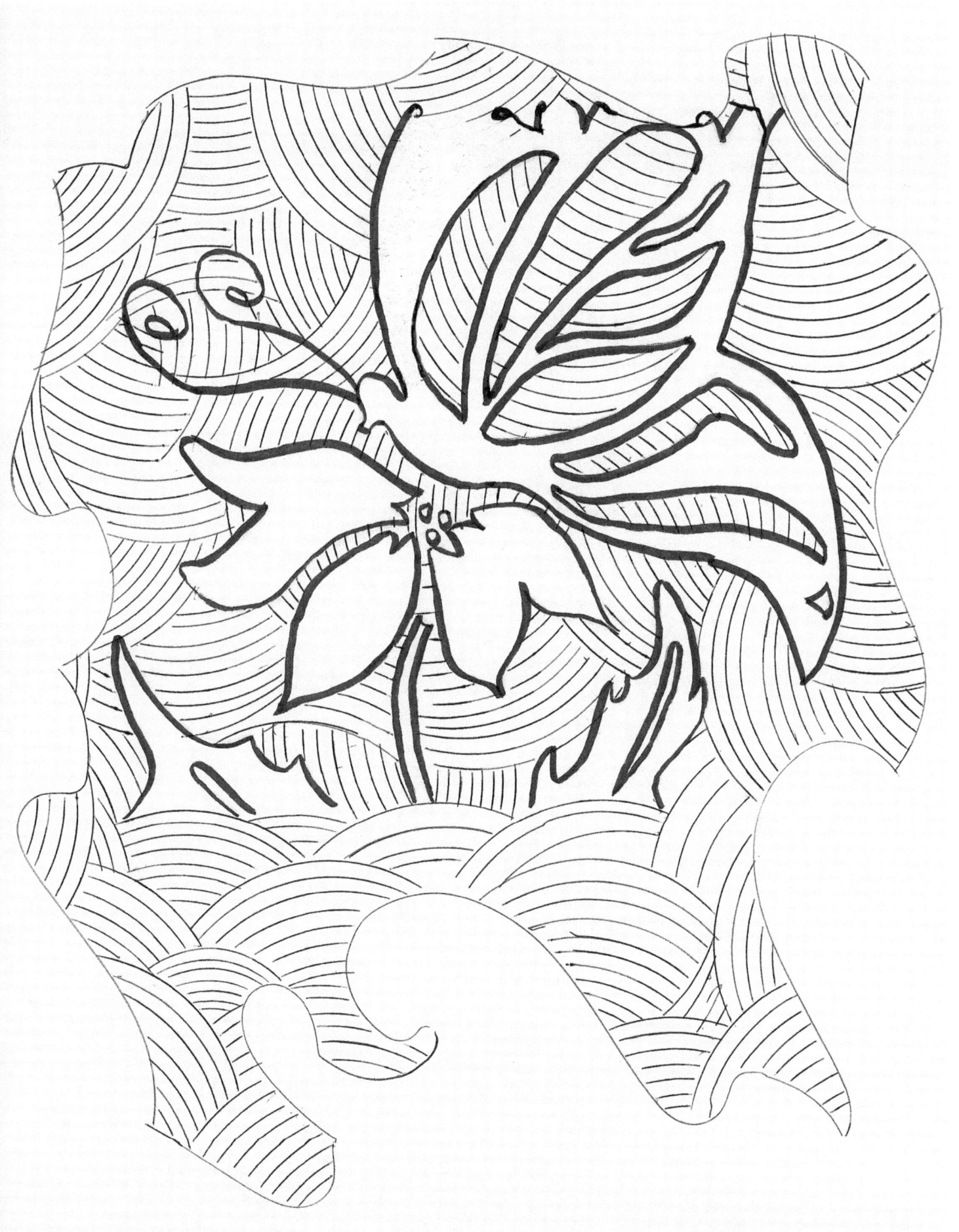

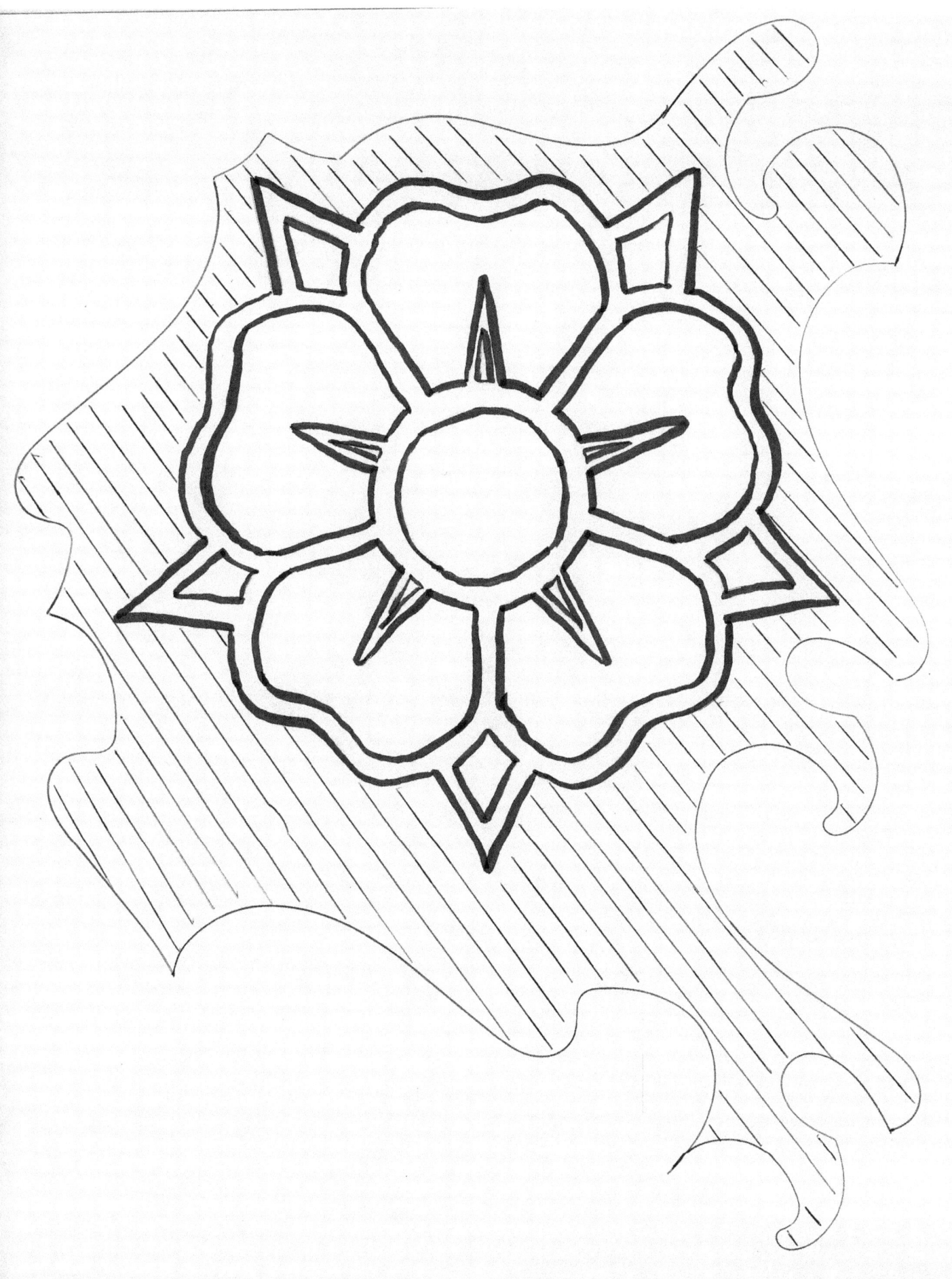

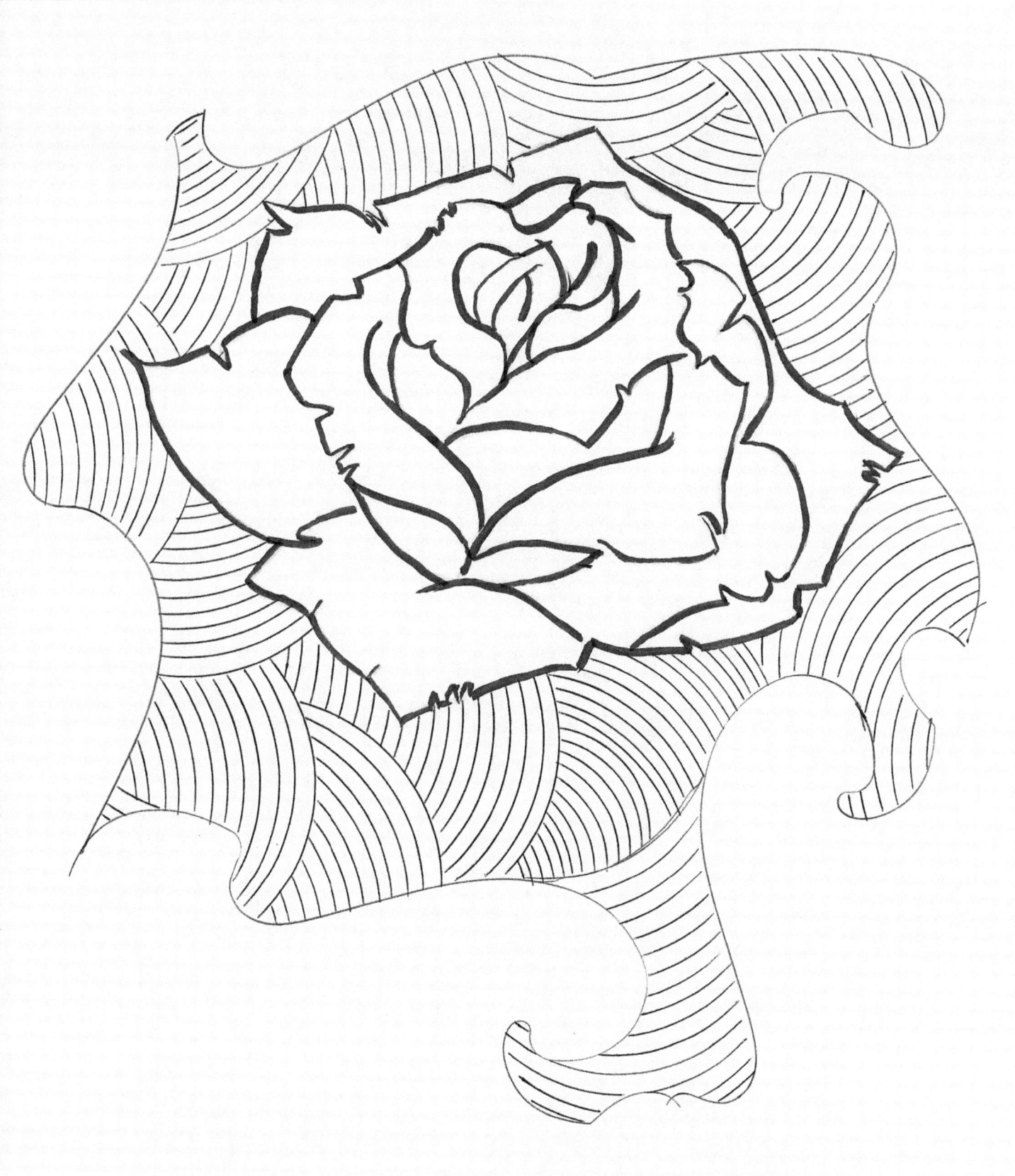

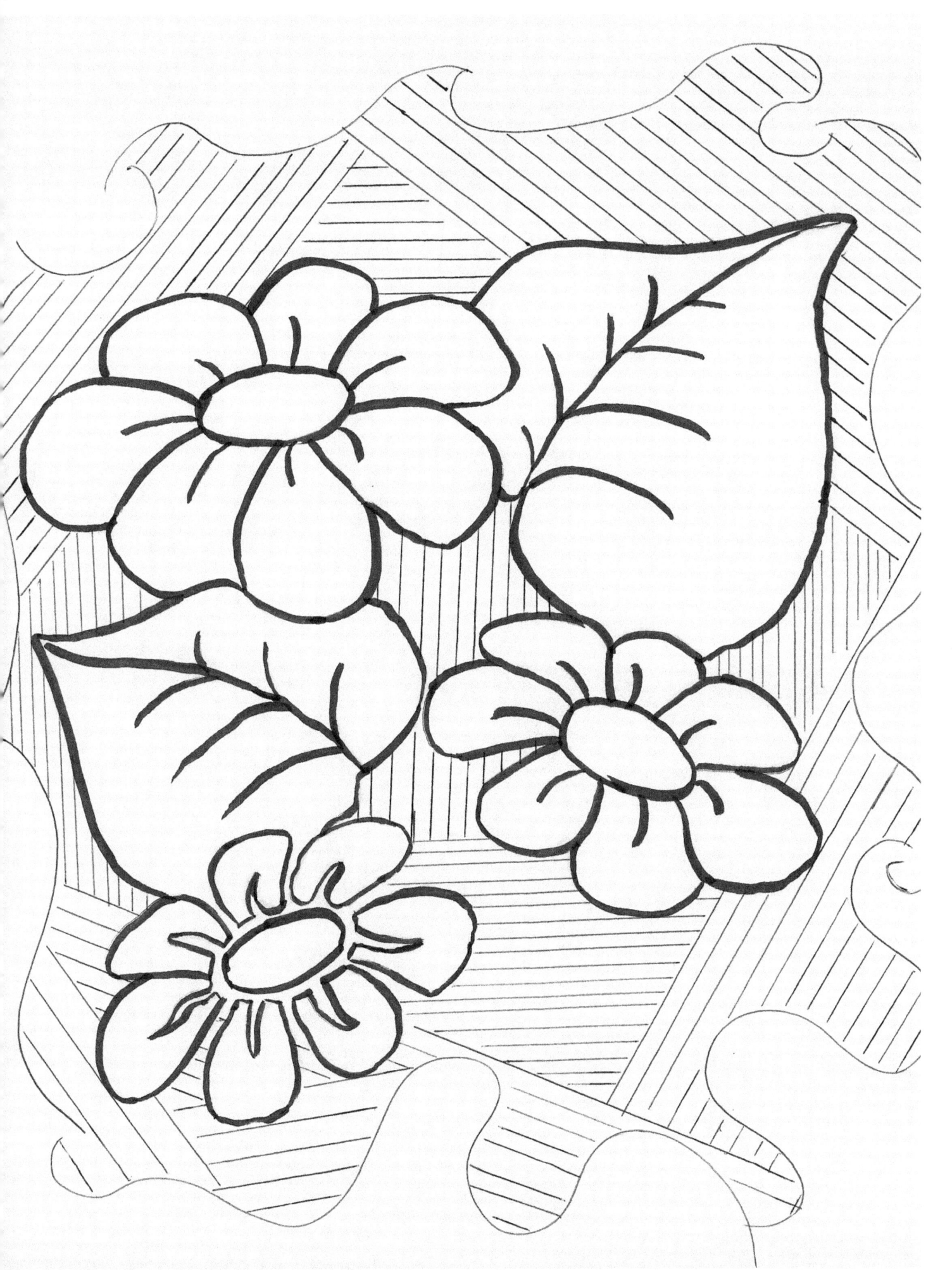

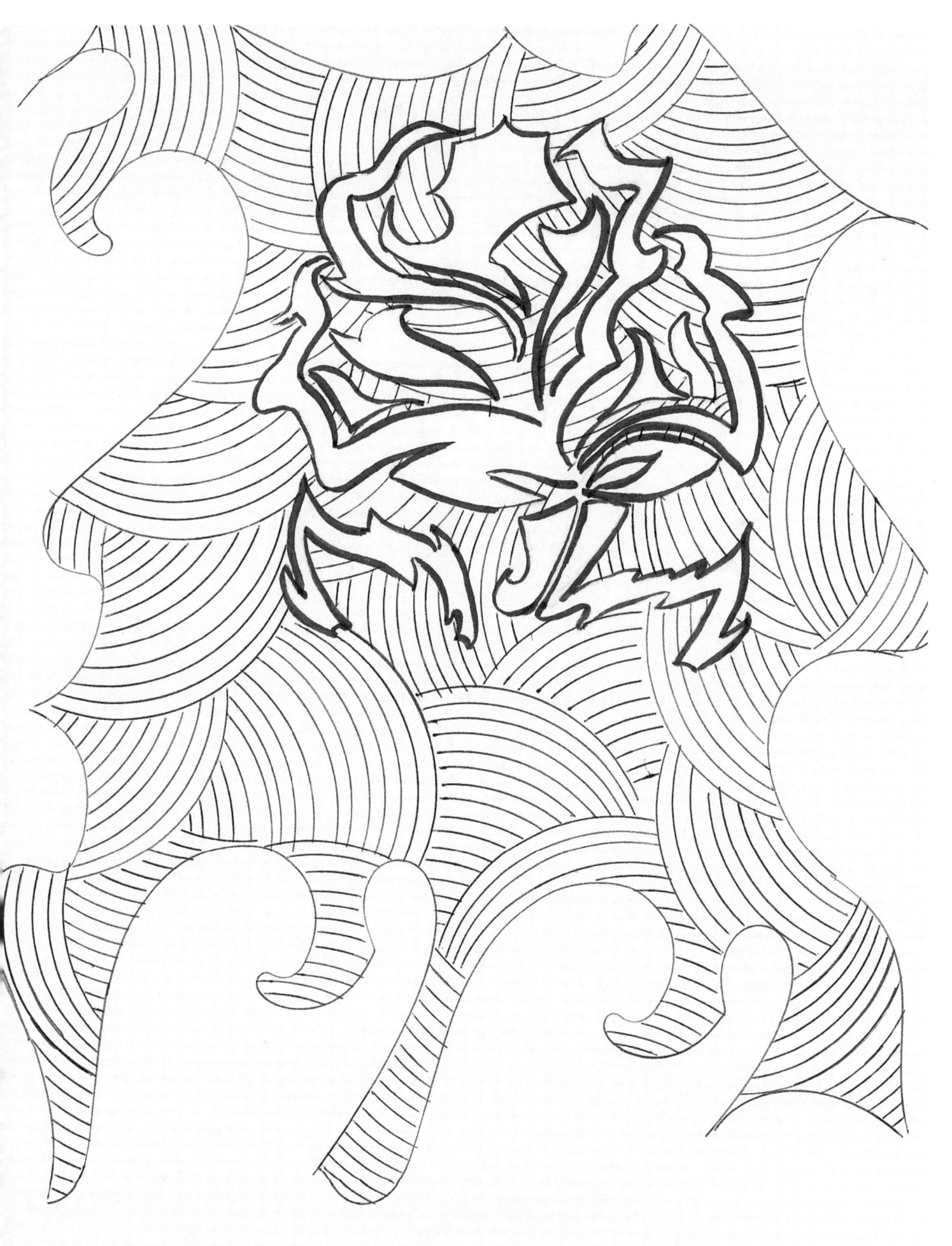

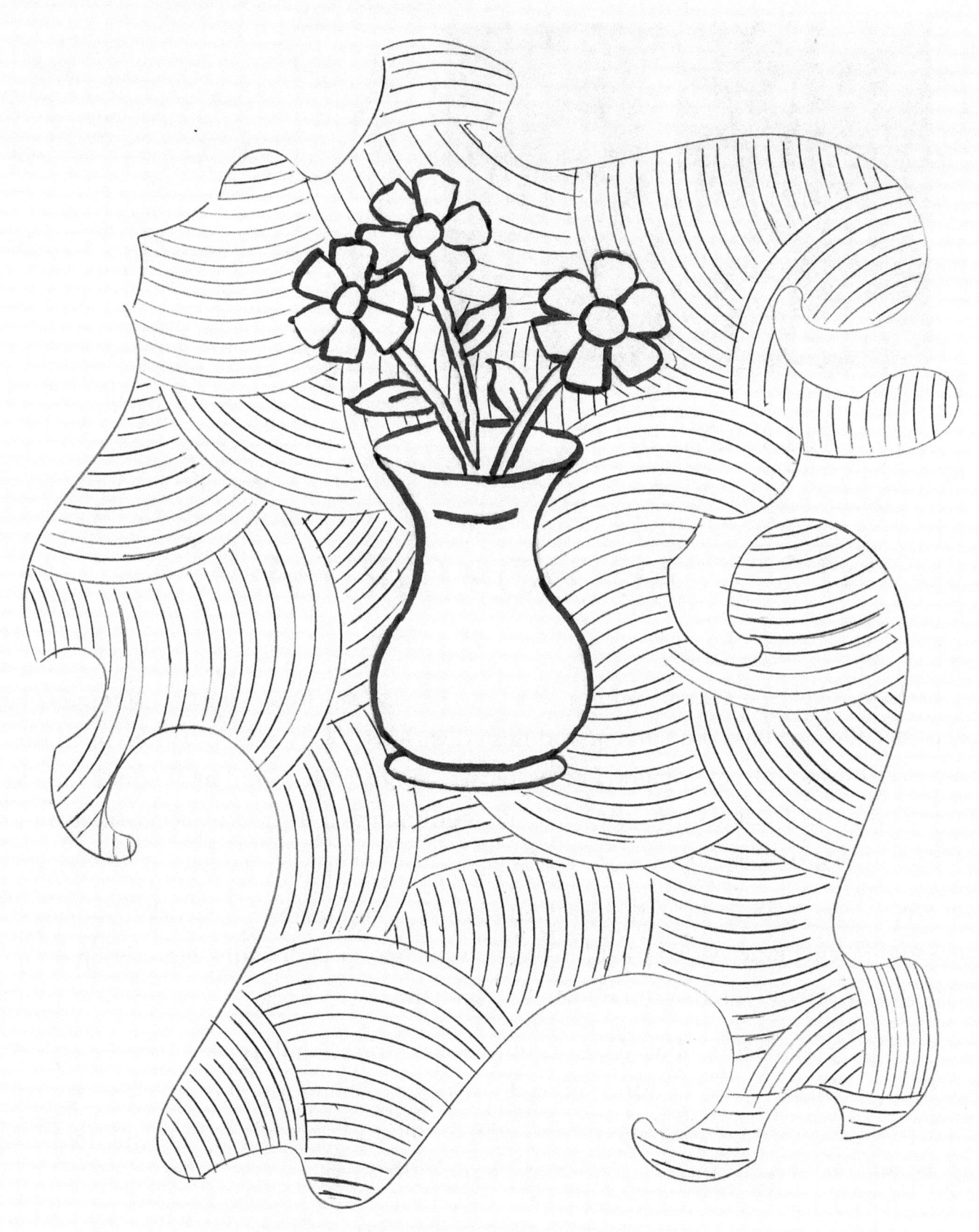

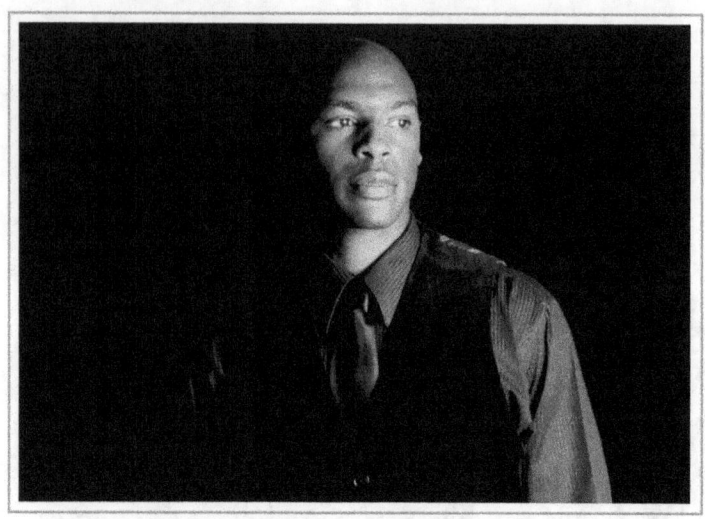

Author/Publisher/Public Speaker

# ABOUT THE AUTHOR/ARTIST

The Los Angeles, Ca based Author/Poet has been performing spoken word poetry for the last decade and has competed in and hosted various poetry slams, cruises, open mic events, locally and internationally. The writer has also been featured in articles spotlighting performances from features, theatre plays, community outreach projects, performing arts programs and workshops.

The Author currently has Poetry books, compact disk, Artwork, Coloring Books and Performance videos that have gone viral and are currently viewed numerous times a day through national and international channels.

The poetic stories have been described as inspirational, powerful and family friendly, most importantly it address everyday aspects of life and offers a different perspective. Through his work Darrell has moved generations, influenced ideas and empowered readers and listeners to enjoy life and achieve their dreams.

www.ingramcontent.com/pod-product-compliance
Lightning Source LLC
Chambersburg PA
CBHW080623180526
45168CB00007B/3035